MOTHER.

Marie Desires

la petite mort

you undressed for
me that night
we lay together,
watched and held
each other,

uttered chaste
praise with
stuttered breaths

as cloth became
skin and skin
became flesh

dusky and pink,
curved and
slender,

i fell as you
watched, as you
came in my arms

together and apart,
limbs formed
roots to ground us

in that moment
and this

for, certain as the
sun rises, i rise
each time you slip
in

under the covers,
beside me,
beneath and above

with each tryst, i
look to you, hold
you

as you writhe into
my soul and out of
my life

say:

what do you see in
my eyes, in my
mind

in my heart as it
crawls its way to
you,

sickly and brittle in
the wake of your
exit

exodus out there
and in here

before me and
them you walked,
danced and left
me,

so, to you i ask
both then and
now:

what do you know
of my love, of my
lust and want,

my desire for you
in every way,
brutal and volatile

twisted but right,
how i begged for
more in the
interim

yet you denied
me.

a prayer of
forgiveness to ease
the longing

each night, when i
grasp myself in
hand and dream
of you

your body, your
mind, your mouth
on me and mine

in the heat of
hands clasped, a
new sex was born

from which i learnt
to bury the old

under the nature
of sin as
forgiveness was left
to burn

in the frozen air,
we loved, and love
lost our sense of
self and unity,

to its grave i went,
and saw you there

i saw you there
and cried.

For you made a
fool of death with
your beauty.

Obituary

See my worth, miss my presence

Shout my praises, regret lost time

Laude me, reminisce

Do it while I live. Not Posthumously.

MOTHER. (This Is Not A Story.)

When I was a child, my mother would brush my hair.

When I was a child, my mother would sit me down, unwrap the towel and give it to me to hold, knowing the damp fabric would be of comfort to me. I'd gather it close and press it tight against my face, taking in the smell of coconut and shea butter from the conditioner. Next came the oils; tea tree and

black castor,
slathered into the
dense curls, before
bunching –

VERB bunching: [1]
collect or fasten
into a compact
group: [2] form or
cause to form tight
folds: "she
bunched sections
of my hair
together in her
hand"

SIMILAR:
bundle/ clump/
gather/ collect :)

– to get the oils to
the roots and ends
of my hair. Then,
as she grabbed the
hairbrush and the
low hum of dryer
started up, she'd

lean down and
whisper

*'I don't want to
hear a word'*

 and I'd close my
eyes and shove the
towel deep into
my mouth as the
hot air hit my
scalp, till it bulged
and I could hardly
swallow, clamping
down tight before
the first wail could
escape.

When I was a
child, my mother
would brush my
hair and my eyes
would scrunch
close from the
pain as the brush
would tear through
my hair.

When I was a
child, my mother
would brush my
hair and I would
sob muffled cries
and scream all the
while.

When I was a
child, my mother
would brush my
hair as she argued
with my father and
I would close my
eyes and pray for
have the sleek
straight hair of the
blond barbies I
played with.

When I was a
child, my mother
would brush my
hair and I would
spend the night
half awake, afraid
to lay my head
down.

Now I am older.

Now I am older, I brush my own hair. I sit in my room with the windows open and welcome in the cool breeze from outdoors. I run my fingers through my hair, wide tooth combs and soft bristle brushes. I never use heat. I never bunch.

Now I am older, I think about putting chemicals in my hair to forcibly make it sleeker. Neater.

Now I am older, I brush my mother's hair. It is thinning

and breaking at
the back. Still no
greys. I gently
separate the
strands and add in
the oils, massaging
it in, even as she
complains it's
taking too long. I
stretch the coils
into plaits to dry,
even as she calls
for the dryer.

Now I am a
mother.

Now I am a
mother, I brush
my daughter's
hair.

Now I am a
mother, I braid my
daughter's kinky
hair and I then I

twist my own. I
don't think of
relaxers or
texturisers.

I do think of the
new dolls with afro
hair and long
braids. I think of
little girls wishing
for the long braids
and coloured
strands, not
knowing of the
pain that hides
behind each style.

Now I am a
mother, my
daughter cries
when I brush her
hair. I kiss her
cheeks softly. I tell
her not to fidget
and I try not to
think of the
hairdryer at the

back of the
bathroom cabinet.

Instead, I think of
my mother.

Hymn for the Weekend.

I pray for the warmth to come early this year.
That I may spend the days out in the sun.
That I may bathe under its lights as my own.
That I may bask in its heat until my skin is
baked.
I pray for the rain to come again before the
year's end.
Let it wash over me, cleanse me from within.
Let it clear the dirt from my home and water
the fruits of tomorrow.
Let it cool the ardours of men, that we return
to the clarity of yesterday's skies.
I pray for a better present, that all gifts be as
generous as today.
I pray in the name of my Lord.

Do not feel you must now say Amen.

Rhyme and Run-Along:

start

emoting

      smoking

         smiting

            igniting

               Ignatius

                  tenacious

voracious

    volatile

       moral-high

           peace-of-mind

      peace-of-cake

  eliminate

anticipate

precipitate

participate

partisan

artisan

artistry

ministry

minister

spinster

sinister

cynical

cyclical

sycamore

spiritual

lyrical

      limital

         limited

            stop.

To Hold the World in My Hands

Morning
squabbles and the
Evening cries,
In the late early
hours of a
summertime night.

Hollowed shadows
etched deep
beneath dark eyes,
Such are the
rewards of a
treasurer's plight.

In the days of old,
kings stood at the
centre,
And mater still
made the fiercest
of knights.

Sitting guard at the
cot lest evil enter,

Her girdle her
only arms in the
heat of the fight.

A mother's love
knows no end and
no bound,
To be latched and
unlatched like a
common cow.

In the humility is
beauty found,
Enough to saddle
up and embrace
the plow.

A mother's love is
true and well
endowed,
Her body
stretched and torn
in the afterbirth.

In the snuffling
cries of mother
and child,
Long months into
laborious pain find
their worth.

I found my place
in the dance old as
time,
The day I carried
you into the world.

So small yet tough,
uniquely you but
still mine,

I knew there
would never be
enough words.

Steady as the days
turn and the years
go by,
The memory
remains and
imprint, a brand.

How can I ever
forget or best
describe,
How it felt to hold
the world in my
hands.

Blue Collar Blues

Dawn breaks the night into day

And I open my eyes to the sun's bourgeoning
rays

The six o'clock shuffle to a bathroom queue

Half grunts at fellow wakers,

Bleary 'how do you do?'s

Roasted beans awaken the mind,

Cool air reinvigorates the soul,

Down to the kitchen we haste,

Grabbing plates, mugs, bowls

7 o'clock rings true,

And I pack up my tools,

Shrug on a jacket, slip on gloves

Jam on hats and toe on boots

Goodbye sweet home

I think as I amble away

From dawn's eager call to dusk's chilling embrace,

One more man serves as fodder in the workman's tale.

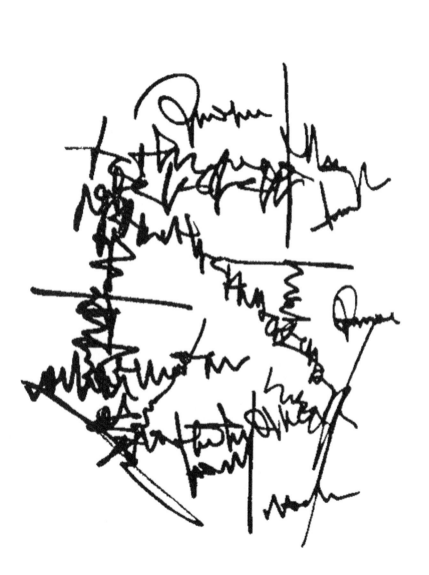

Printed in Great Britain
by Amazon

33563651R00020